AURORA
Art Glass Images
by Thomas Morin, II

With an Introduction on Enlarging, Reshaping, and Simplifying Designs by Trudy Thomas

ISBN 0-913417-03-3

Aurora Publications
6214 Meridian Avenue
San Jose, CA 95120
(408) 997-0437

TABLE OF CONTENTS

AUTHOR'S DEDICATION

To my mother, without whose love, help, encouragement, and inspiration, this book would not have been possible.

PUBLISHER'S FOREWORD

We hope that you will find this book to be a little different. We intended it that way.

The first thing you should notice is that all of the designs in this book look very real. Although these are designs for stained glass, they don't have that stained glass look. The artist, Thomas Morin II, has been able to integrate the lead lines into the designs so effectively that they are hardly noticed. Mr. Morin has also made very few compromises in respect to how the glass likes to be cut, yet the designs can be cut.

Another salient feature of these designs is that they are very rich in detail. The detail not only adds to the beauty of the windows, but also lends them their air of realism.

Stained glass windows, by their very nature, are flat. But there is nothing flat about these windows. Mr. Morin has imbued each design with a strong sense of perspective which gives the windows a feeling of depth rarely found in the stained glass world.

Yes, this book has birds and flowers in it, but not of the usual stained glass variety. These are shown where they live, as if caught in a secret moment by the eye of an artistic camera. But there is more.

Mr. Morin has gone beyond the ordinary. You will find images in the pages of this book which will introduce you to a new world of stained glass imagination. The Still Lifes are especially striking in this respect. The Banana Split Sundae will make your mouth water. The Champagne & Candle Stick will put you in a romantic mood. The Pancakes and Coffee Breakfast will make an early riser out of you.

In addition to their natural beauty, these windows also have great commercial potential for the professional studio. Clients will love these designs in their Ice Cream Parlors, Restaurants, Cocktail Lounges, Liquor Stores, and Wine Tasting Rooms. Of course, home owners will also pay dearly to have one of these gems placed in their kitchen, dining room, or family room bar.

These designs are intended to be at least two feet in diameter, which is about three times their original size. Most of them can be enlarged much beyond that size and still be very manageable in execution. They can also be done in a smaller size, especially if lead lines are removed.

These stained glass designs were not created for beginners. Mr. Morin had the professional and the dedicated hobbiest in mind when he put his pen to paper. They often have many pieces. Some will demand the utmost in skill and experience to cut as conceived and drawn. But they all can be done by a skilled stained glass craftsperson.

But the novice should not shun the opportunity to work with these beautiful designs. The designs can be altered to meet the level of skill of the individual. Lead lines can be removed to reduce the number of pieces. Others can be added to simplify the cutting. These designs can accept a great deal of alteration because they are so rich in detail, and because the artist has made every line count. If one removes some lines, the remainder will support and maintain the design.

Before working on a project, we suggest that you make a copy of the design and fill in all the colors with colored pencils. This will help you in selecting the type and quantity of glass you will need for the project. Also, it is difficult to identify some of the detail in some of the more complex designs; by filling in the colors of the more obvious elements, you will be better able to correctly identify the various details of the design.

To help guide the beginner, and some experts also, in adapting these designs to their requirements, we have included an introduction on enlarging, re-shaping, simplifying, and adapting these designs to a variety of situations and needs. This section has been written by Trudy Thomas, a craftsperson of vast experience and the author of "Decorative Soldering for Stained Glass, Jewelry, and Other Crafts."

Mr. Morin has been doing stained glass for several years. He is currently studying art at the University of Rhode Island in Kingston, Rhode Island. His home is in San Jose, California. When not at college, he works with his mother in her stained glass studio in San Jose.

We hope you enjoy this book as much as we did in creating it.

Ken Churilla
Publisher

INTRODUCTION

The designs in this book offer the stained glass craftsperson a chance to create finished pieces with a unique realism. Mr. Morin has developed projects with a broad variety of subject matter and he has paid special attention to detail in each design.

The advantages of a design book of this broad scope are many. The designs may be executed exactly as shown only enlarged to suit a specific application. they also can be used as a basic framework from which to work. Areas may be added, deleted or modified to suit the needs of any craftsperson.

The craftsperson may modify these designs to suit their individual needs and abilities. the information contained in this text will give you instructions on how to successfully modify any design. I will tell you how to enlarge or reduce a design size. You will learn how to alter the shape of the finished window from the basic design as given. You will see how to add or remove cut lines to simplify your pattern. Some of the most popular methods of pattern enlargement will be discussed in detail. There is also a section on the importance of glass and color selection in a project.

ALTERING THE SIZE OF DESIGNS 2

As you can see these designs are too small to execute as shown. You will need to enlarge them to fit your specific application. There are many ways to enlarge the designs in this book.

One of the easiest ways is to have a graphics or blueprint shop do it for you. This is often quite costly, but it is quick and easy. They can usually reproduce anything in a series of enlarging duplications. The finished enlargement is completely accurate, yet, because of the method used, they cannot always be enlarged to any dimension that you specify. They must work within the mathematical progressions of their equipment. They usually double dimensions each time; a 4x4 thus becomes an 8x8, then 16x16, and then 32x32. If you want a 36x36 you would be out of luck, unless you add a 2" border to each edge. Adding a border strip is a good way to slightly modify the size of any pattern.

Remember, if you have a pattern photographically enlarged, you are also having the cutlines enlarged. You must reduce the thickness of these lines when making your cutting pattern. Use a felt tip pen that produces $1/8$" lines for lead work or a ball point pen for copper foil projects. The use of proper thickness of pattern lines is essential in the successful execution of your project.

Another method for enlarging a design to any size pattern is by the use of a projector. A design in this book may be removed and placed in an opaque projector and its image projected onto a paper taped to a wall in front of the projector. If your projector will not accommodate an original as large as those given in this book you may need to have it reduced. This can easily be done at most shops where printing is done. Many offices, libraries and schools have these copiers too. We generally have a 64% reduction made, this size seems to fit most projectors.

Draw the desired outside borders of the finished pattern onto the pattern paper before attaching it to the wall. Use a right angle to insure that corners are square where necessary. If you are enlarging a design to fit within a circle you must draw an accurately round circle. If you do not have a beam compass you must improvise. We have found that a length of common jack chain, a long push pin, and a narrow tipped ball point pen will do the trick. Firmly secure one end of the chain to the center of the desired circle. Measure out along the chain until you have reached the desired radius ($1/2$ the diameter) of the circle you want to draw. Place your pen into that link. Pulling outward against that link, holding the pen vertical, carefully rotate the pen around the center point pin until the circle has been drawn. The circle should be very accurate as long as the pen is held vertical and the center point pin does not move. Accurate pre-bordering is important as it gives you something to center into when adjusting the projector, thus assuring a finished pattern that is exactly the size and shape desired.

Adjust the projector so that the image projected on the wall is properly positioned within the pre-drawn finished borders. Care should be taken to keep the projector level and straight as this will eliminate distortion of the projected image, see Fig. 1.

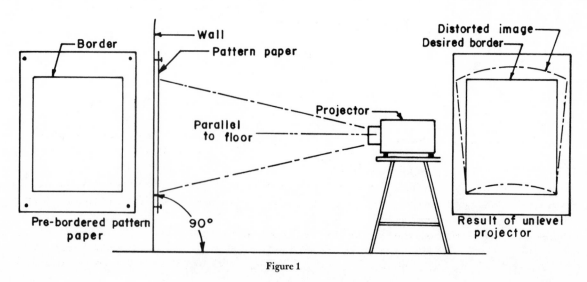

Figure 1

Once the image has been adjusted to the desired size, simply trace the projected image lines with a pencil. The finished drawing will be an exact duplication of the original, but larger. Remember to be sure that all desired lines have been traced before turning off and/or moving the projector.

These projectors are available for use at most schools, libraries and stained glass stores. They are easy to use and most patterns can be reproduced in less than a half hour.

If you have access to an overhead transparent projector rather than an opaque projector, it can be used in much the same way. The original design from this book can easily be reproduced as a transparency. Most facilities that have such a projector will have the equipment for making transparencies too. The same procedures should be followed for tracing the enlarged image on the pattern paper as described above.

If none of the projectors listed above are available and you have a camera that will take slide pictures you can do a similar method of enlargement. This method is often used when creating an original design too. Simply photograph the subject (using slide film) and have it processed. The slide may then be projected with a slide projector onto the pre-bordered pattern attached to the wall and the image traced. If you are using this method to create an original pattern from a photographic subject simply trace the basic images and add cut lines where necessary.

Another popular way to enlarge designs is by the "grid method." This requires some artistic ability and patience. An original design is overlayed with a piece of transparent grid or graph paper ($\frac{1}{4}$ inch grid is easy to begin with for very large enlargements). A larger grid is drawn on a piece of pattern paper to the desired finished dimension of the enlarged design. The size of the large grid is determined by how large you want the finished drawing. If your original is 4x4 and you desire a finished drawing 16x16 your original grid size should be $\frac{1}{4}$ inch squares and your enlarged grid should use 1 inch squares. This means that you are making the new drawing 4 times larger than the original.

This is calculated by dividing the desired final dimension (16) by the original dimension (4) which results in a ratio of 4. Then multiply the ratio (4) by the size of the original grid ($\frac{1}{4}$) which in this case results in $\frac{4}{4}$ or 1 inch. This means that each $\frac{1}{4}$ inch square of the original pattern will equal 1 inch on the enlarged pattern, see Fig. 2.

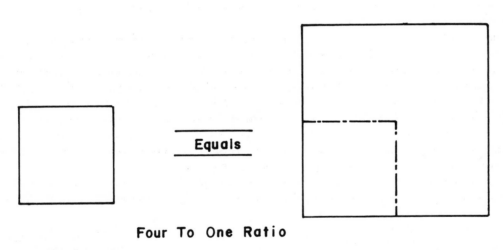

Four To One Ratio

Figure 2

Once the grid has accurately been drawn on your new pattern paper you begin to transfer lines from the original to the new. You draw everything in the $\frac{1}{4}$ inch square in its same position onto the 1 inch square, only 4 times larger. BE SURE TO AC-CURATELY REPRODUCE THE POSITIONING.

If everything is done properly you will have an accurate reproduction 4 times larger than the original. As you are drawing on the enlarged grid keep checking the overall picture to see that you are maintaining the design. Do not become so involved with the lines that you lose sight of the overall design.

Fig. 3 shows an example of this method, notice the new drawing is the same only larger.

The original design dimension is $1\frac{1}{2}$ inch, the desired final dimension is 3 inches. The original grid is $\frac{1}{2}$ inch. We calculated the final grid size by dividing 3 by $1\frac{1}{2}$, which equals 2. We then multiplied 2 by $\frac{1}{2}$ which gave us a final grid size of 1 inch.

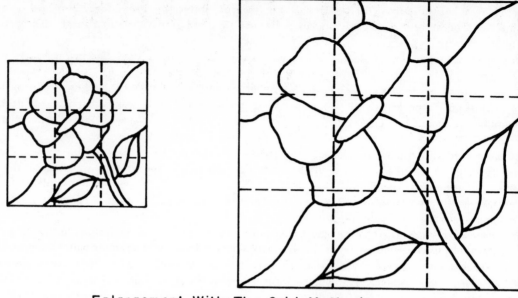

Enlargement With The Grid Method

Figure 3

Another enlarging technique requires a pantograph. This is a drafting tool that is used to enlarge designs. The finished enlargement is accurate yet somewhat shaky inline quality. You may have to go back later and improve the line quality. Pantographs can be purchased at most graphics or art supply stores. They come with good instructions and are a handy tool to have if you do a lot of enlargements and you do not have easy access to a projector. Fig. 4 shows the basic set up of a pantograph.

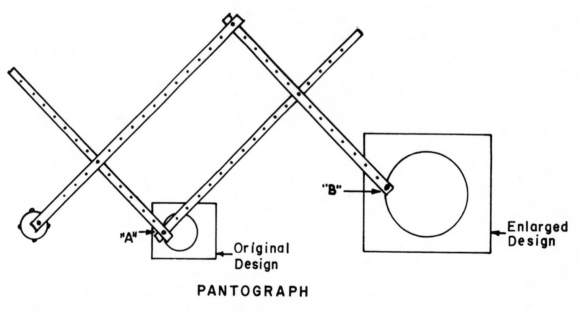

PANTOGRAPH

Figure 4

A pantograph is a set of 4 hinged bars, which are made with corresponding calibrated holes. If you follow the instructions you can set the pantograph to many different degrees of enlargement. The original drawing is placed under point "A" of the tool. As the "A" pointer is traced along the lines on the original design, the lines are reproduced in an enlarged version under the pencil point at point "B" of the tool. The drawing is reproduced accurately by the pencil at point "B'." This reproduction is accurate although somewhat shaky in line quality. You can simply trace over these lines to smooth them out if necessary.

ALTERING THE SHAPE OF DESIGNS 3

There are times when you will have a drawing that is almost but not quite the right shape of a project that you want to build. You may also find a design that contains subject matter that is similar to what you want to build. It is often quite helpful to go through a design book, such as this, to find ideas for your current project. Learn to look for overall concept rather than a specific size or shape. It is relatively simple to convert the size or shape of almost any design. If you realize this when you begin to search for a design to fit within a specific window you will be able to consider the designs of many more patterns for content rather than just its shape. You will no longer have to limit your search to originally square patterns to fit your square project.

With a little bit of ingenuity and some artistic talent you can alter almost any design to fit your need. The techniques described in the following section can save you much time and frustration, not to mention many hours of original design time.

I described earlier how to add a border to enlarge a design slightly. This is frequently done if only minor enlargements are to be made to the size of a pattern, such as up to 4 inches.

You may also reduce most full size patterns slightly by moving the borders inward an inch or so. You must be careful though so as not to jeopardize the content of the design. You may have to do a little art work to clean up the new borders.

The overall shape of a design can be altered too. If you want to make a circular or oval pattern into a square or rectangular pattern, there are two methods that can be used. First, add "squaring corners" with or without borders. "Squaring corners" are pieces of glass that are cut along lines that are projected outward from the center of a circle or oval, at right angles (90 degrees) to each other shown in Figure 5, Angle "A."

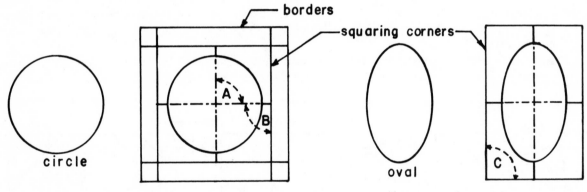

Figure 5

The resulting lines divide the circle or oval into quarter sections. These lines are then connected by perpendicular (90 degrees) lines (Angle "B"), which meet at Angle "C" forming a squared corner. Figure 5 shows typical conversions of circles or ovals to squares or rectangles

The length of the projected lines in Figure 5 determines the finished size of the window. If you do not wish to increase the basic size of the window do not project these lines beyond the edges of the original circle or oval. Simply draw the perpendicular lines from the point where the projected lines meet the edge of the circle or oval. If you wish to increase the overall dimension by two inches you would terminate the projected lines at one inch from the points where they cross through the outside edge of the circle or oval. the perpendiculars are then drawn from this point.

Additional size can be added by the addition of border strips and/or bevels at each side. When adding squaring corners or borders, remember to use neutral and/or complimentary colors. Do not overpower the subject matter of the main portion of the window.

If you feel a little more artistic you can change a circle into a square by actually extending the lines of the drawing to meet the new borders of your squared window. You may even want to add a little additional artwork, if you feel so inclined, (see Fig. 6).

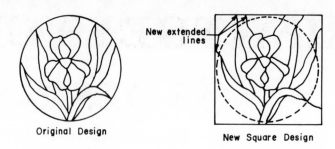

Figure 6

Figure 7 shows how a circular or square pattern can be elongated to form an oval or rectangular pattern with the addition or extension of cut lines. Note that we have added a little artwork to fill the additional space and or maintain the integrity of the design. We also added new elements to balance the design.

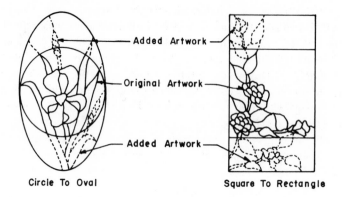

Figure 7

Almost any design can be converted to any size or shape that you might desire. If you learn to envision basic designs in different formats you will achieve the greatest benefits from a design book like this. Remember though, you may have extensive artwork to do with some transformations.

Circles and octagons can be drawn within a square window with a little modification too. Care should be taken not to disrupt the subject matter of the design. Fig. 8 shows two successful transformations. Note that the subject matter of the design was not compromised.

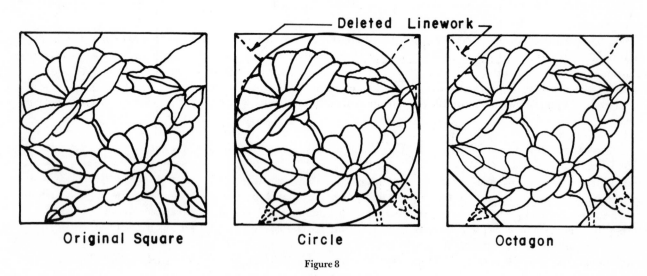

Figure 8

SIMPLIFYING DESIGNS

Once the size and shape of your pattern has been established you need to determine the number and types of cuts that you want. The designs in this book have many lines because they are designed to be enlarged by at least a factor of three. They have enough cut lines to insure workable size pieces on larger windows (22"x34" or larger). The large number of pieces allow the craftsperson to achieve the great number of color variations and detail in nature.

On projects that do not require great enlargement or a high degree of complexity you may want to reduce the number of pieces from the original design. If you use glass that has great color variations and good grain within the glass you can eliminate some of the cut lines and pieces without impacting the original design very much. Figure 9 shows the original design in drawing A. Drawing B shows slight modification by the reduction of some pieces. Note that the subject matter has not been materially changed. Drawing C shows great simplification through the deletion of many lines, yet the subject matter remains intact. Drawing C could be executed in a 12" format and have easily handled pieces. The great detail in Drawing A would, however, require a much larger format to accommodate the number of pieces.

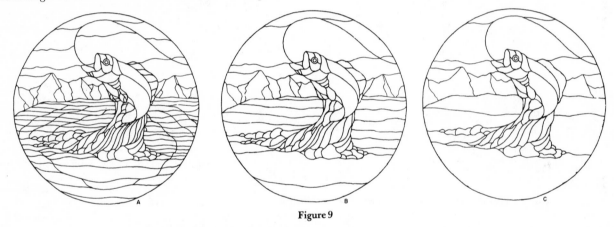

Figure 9

The reduction of the number of pieces will not only make the project easier, but will enable you to work it into a smaller format without having unworkable small pieces or jeopardizing the artistic value of the piece. Many flowers, birds and skyscapes, when done very large, need fine detail or many cuts to adequately show the fine detail and subtle color changes in nature.

When a design is reduced in size you often need to eliminate some of the cut lines. This will reduce the number of small pieces in your project. This is shown in Figure 10. You can often cut one piece to represent many pieces in nature. A flower that has

Figure 10

many petals can often be successfully represented in glass with significantly fewer pieces. One piece can be cut to represent several small details in a pattern that was meant for great enlargement. Figure 10 shows a pattern (A) of a hummingbird that is meant to be done in a much larger format, at least 21'' in diameter, and a much simplified version (B) that can be done as small as 10.''

Note that in Figure 10 (B), the subject matter has remained the same yet many individual feathers have been condensed into a few pieces that successfully represent the detail of the wings or tail of the bird. The flowers and leaves have likewise been altered to achieve simplification without compromising content. In the next section we detail how to choose and use glass to represent the fine details in nature.

The feeling of the subject matter, as well as the number of pieces used can be altered in some cases by totally eliminating things from the design. In Fig. 11 we have removed many cut lines in the ocean and we have entirely removed the volcano and volcanic cloud. This not only significantly reduces the number of pieces, but changes the whole mood of the design. Feel free to exercise your creativity to make the design truly your own.

ORIGINAL   REVISION

Figure 11

All of the designs in this book have workable cuts, however some will require patience and experience in their execution. Tight inside curves require you to gradually remove the unwanted glass from the area. You may have to score and remove the glass from the curve a little at a time.

Many of you may feel the need to add additional cut lines to make the project easier. Remember though that there are very few unnecessary lines in nature. Please do not get into the habit of adding too many cut lines just to make your life easier, challenge yourself. Figure 12 shows a design, as given in this book and with proper modification. Note that with the addition of only 2 cut lines at the tail of the eagle we have greatly simplified the cutting of the background.

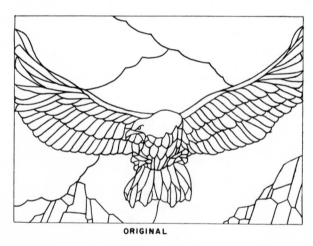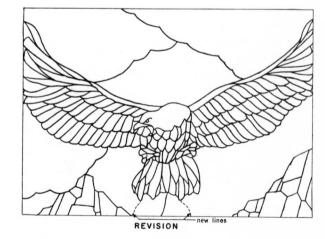

ORIGINAL   REVISION — new lines

Figure 12

SELECTING GLASS 5

In the previous section I have made frequent mention of proper glass selection. The glass that you use in a window is one of the most important elements with which you will have to deal. You should not only consider the color, but the texture and tint of the glass to be used. Much of the fine detail present in nature can be achieved with the proper glass selection.

Always be aware of the natural appearance of what you are trying to reproduce in glass and select your glass accordingly. Always run the grain of the glass along the same lines that nature flows. Clouds usually run horizontally in nature, therefore, cut the glass so that its grain runs horizontally. Pay special attention to the graining and color variations when selecting the glass. For example, the grain of leaves runs diagonally outward from the center vein toward the tip of the leaf (See Fig. 13).

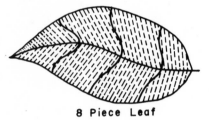

8 Piece Leaf

Figure 13

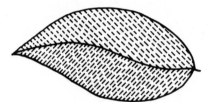

Good Glass Grain Selection

Figure 14

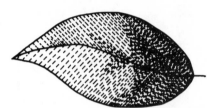

Good Grain and Color Variation

Figure 15

Always be consistent with grain selection when cutting the pieces. The realism of the finished window depends on the care you take when cutting.

Often the proper use of glass grain can enable you to eliminate some cut lines, simplifying your project while not endangering the realism of your project. The leaf in Figure 14 shows how the leaf in Figure 13 has been cut in only two pieces yet maintains a good level of realism. The graining in the glass now represents the veins of the leaf.

If you want to add even more realism, you can carefully choose the exact areas within the glass, paying special attention to the grain and color variations. Leaves are generally darker at the base and lighter near the tip. If you can cut your glass right, you can use the color change as well as the grain of the glass to further enhance the realism of a piece (See Fig. 15).

Remember to use these grain and color variations in many places within your window. Most sheets of glass have good color variations within themselves. You should always buy a little more glass than absolutely necessary in order to insure the proper use of color change and grain. It is just as easy to cut a piece with the right grain and color as the wrong. The difference between a window with well thought out coloration and use of grain from one without it is quite significant.

With what you have read in this introduction you should be able to take the designs in this book or any other book and use them to their fullest. You should no longer have to look at a design within the format that it has been drawn. You should be able to consider the content only and adapt it to your special needs. This gives the craftsperson great flexibility as well as creativity when looking at or selecting designs.

TM-1   Rose Bouquet

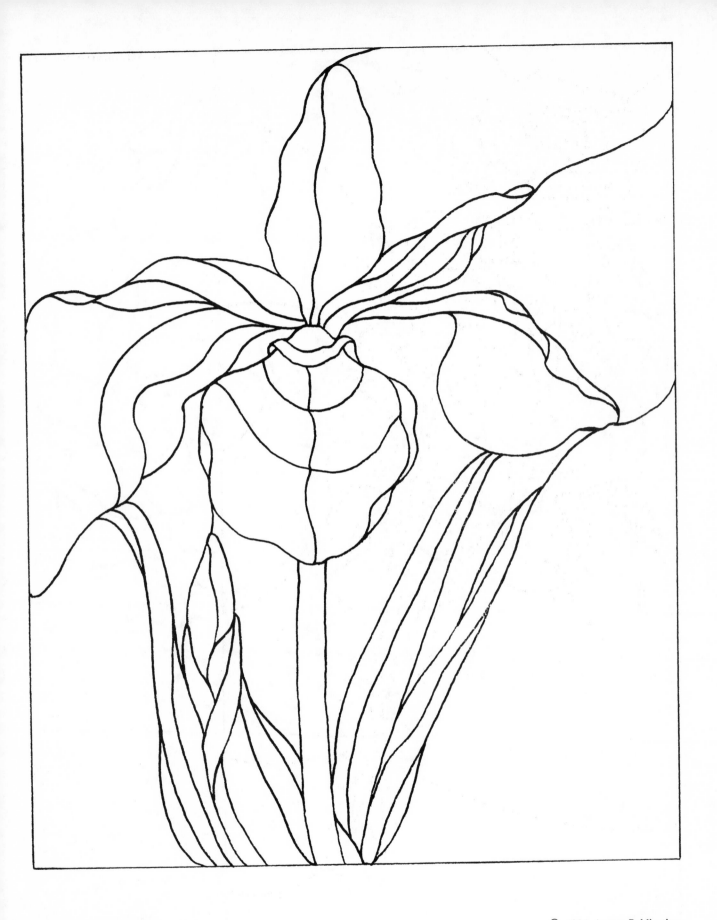

TM-2   Iris Sibirica

TM-3   Peonies I

12

TM-4   Gladiolus, Colville

TM-5   Marvel of Peru

14

TM-6   Day Lily

TM-7   **Southern Magnolia Flowers**

TM-8   Morning Glories

TM-9   Morning Glories Climbing

TM-10   Bird of Paradise Flower I

TM-11 Madonna Lily of Leonardo de Vinci

TM-12   Water Lily and Butterfly

TM-13   Camellia

TM-14   Three Irises of different colors

TM-15 Tulips dancing

© 1985, Aurora Publications

24

TM-16   Tulip Patch

TM-17   Bird of Paradise II

TM-18   Campanula Latifolia

27

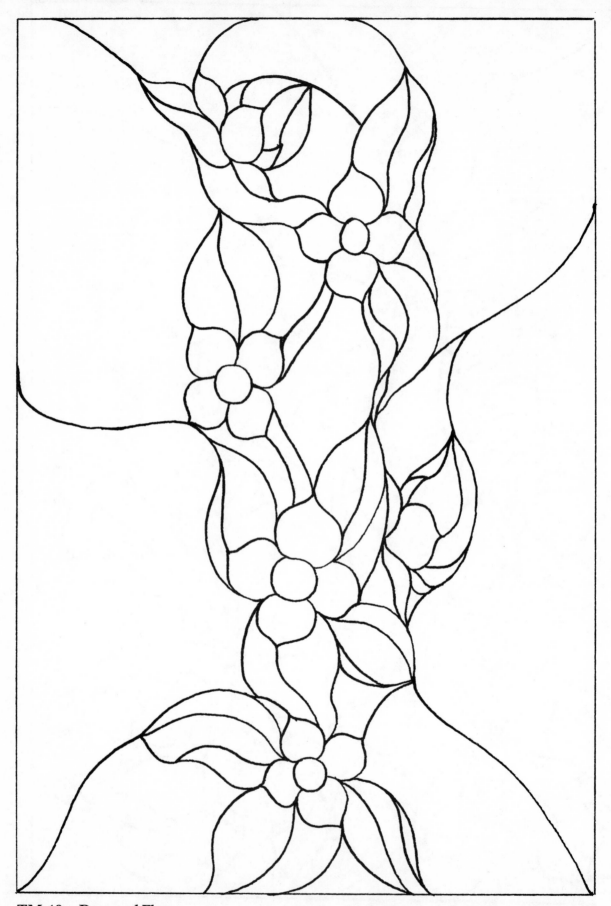

TM-19   Dogwood Flowers

TM-20   Peonies II   © 1985, Aurora Publications

TM-21   Lily Patch

TM-22   Hummingbird and Morning Glories

TM-23   Toucan in Jungle

TM-24   Flamingo Couple in water

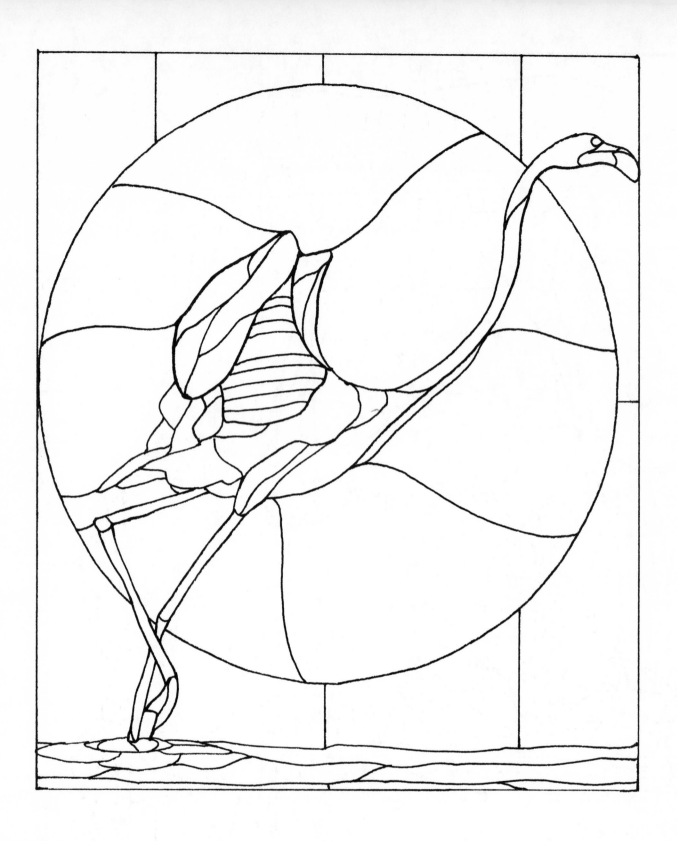

TM-25   Flamingo taking off

TM-26   Mallard Ducks Feeding

© 1985, Aurora Publications

TM-27   Swan Standing in a Pond

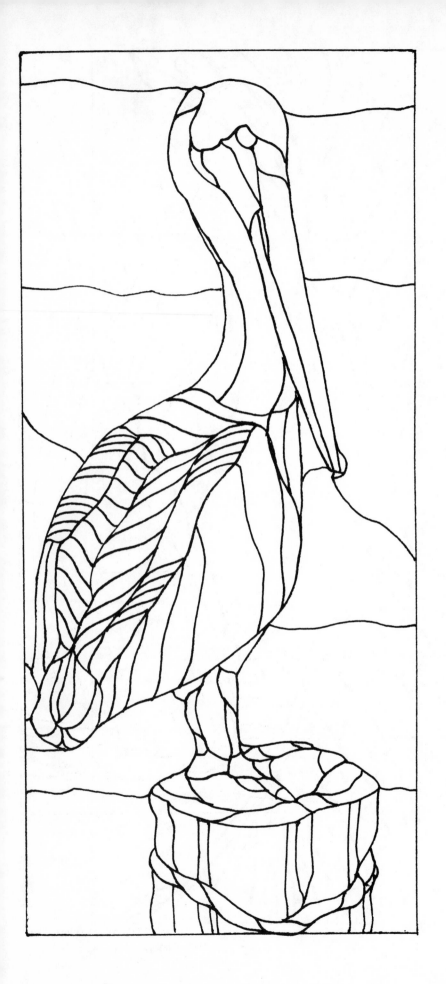

TM-28   Pelican on Post

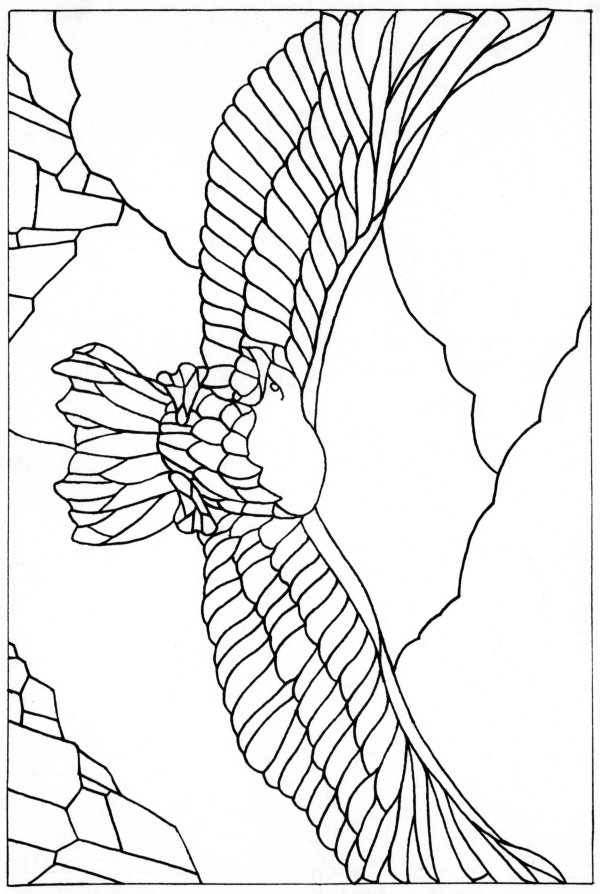

TM-29   Eagle in Flight

TM-30   Eagle Landing

TM-31 Eagle's Head

TM-32 Owl in Tree

© 1985, Aurora Publications

TM-33   Owl Attack

TM-34   Fish Jumping

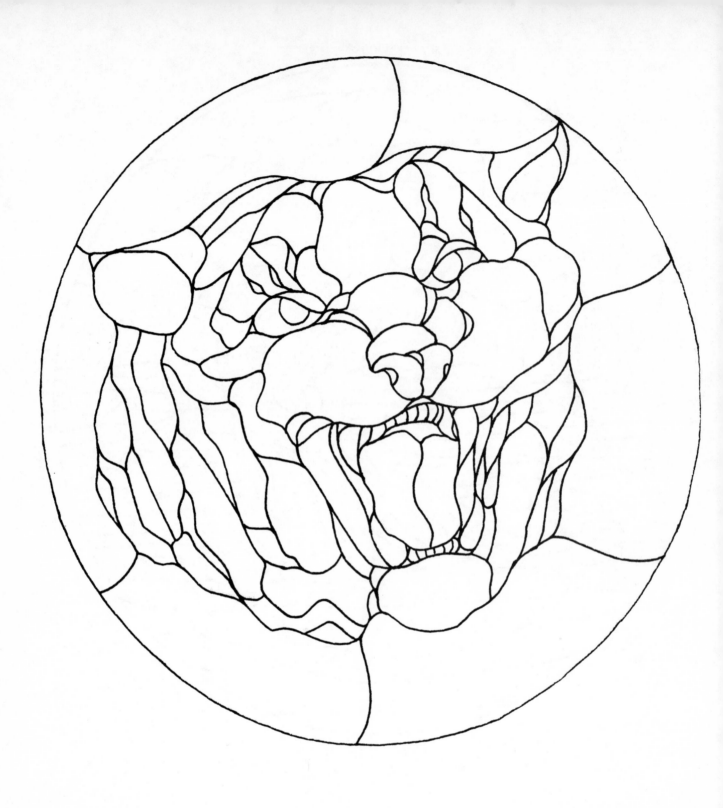

TM-35   Tiger's Head

TM-36   Stag's Head

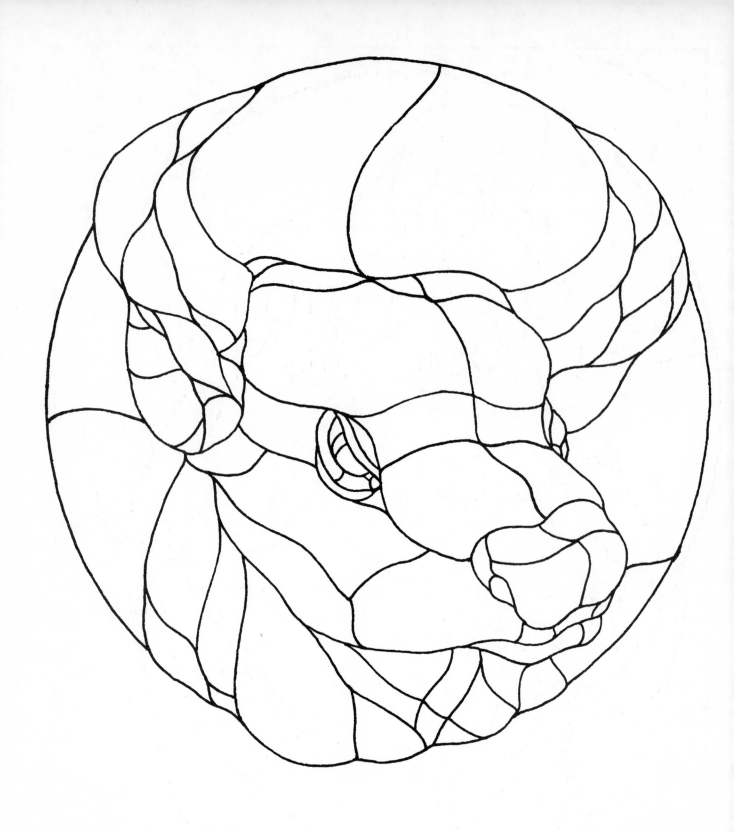

TM-37 Bull's Head

TM-38   Horse's Head

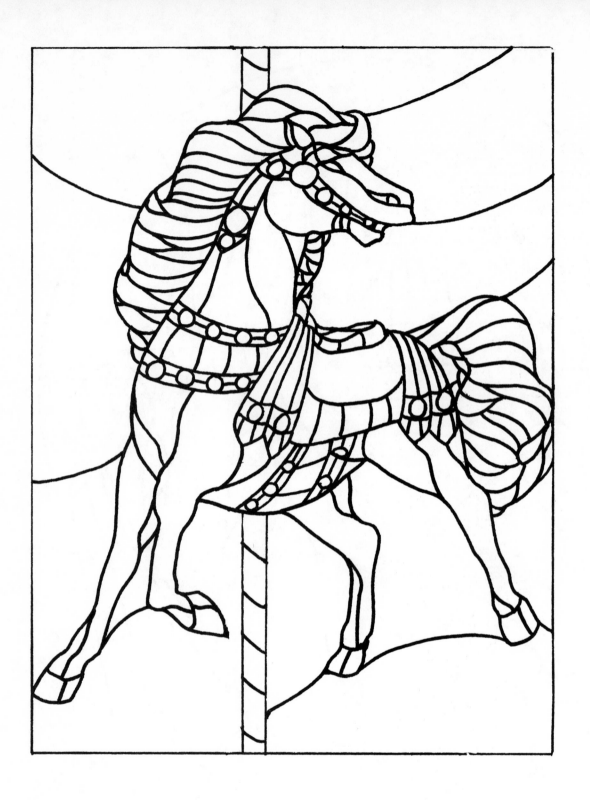

TM-39   Carousel Horse Turning

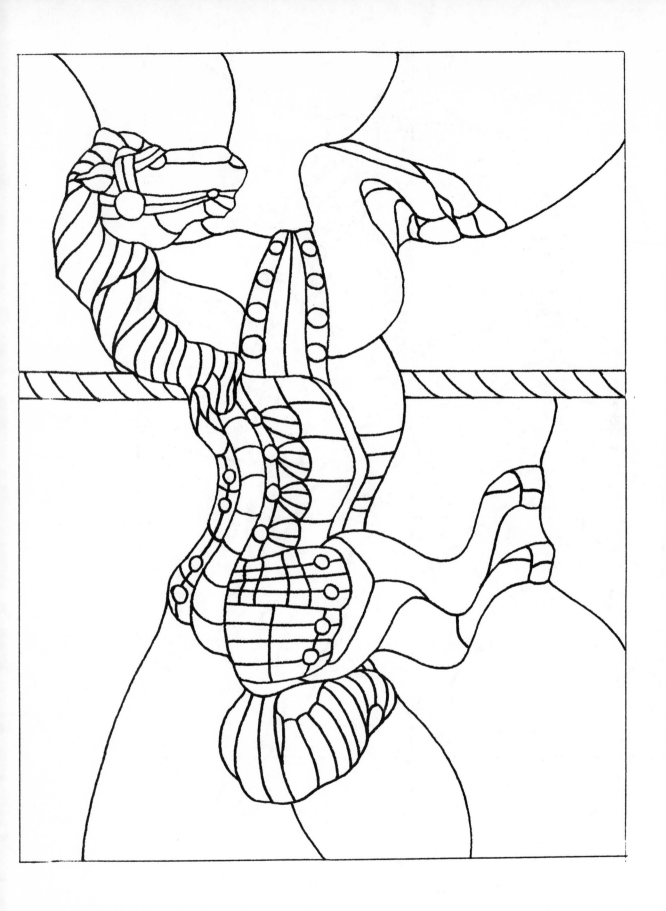

TM-40   Carousel Horse in Profile

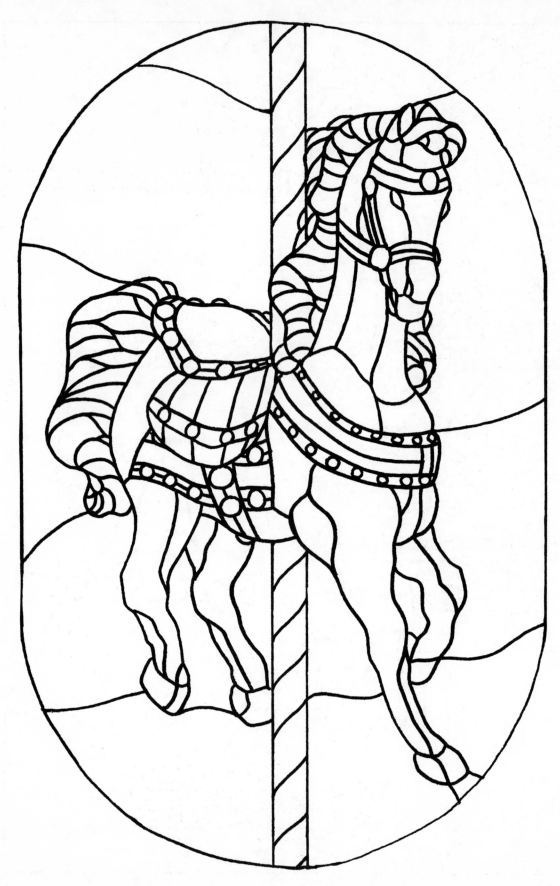

TM-41   Carousel Horse Approaching

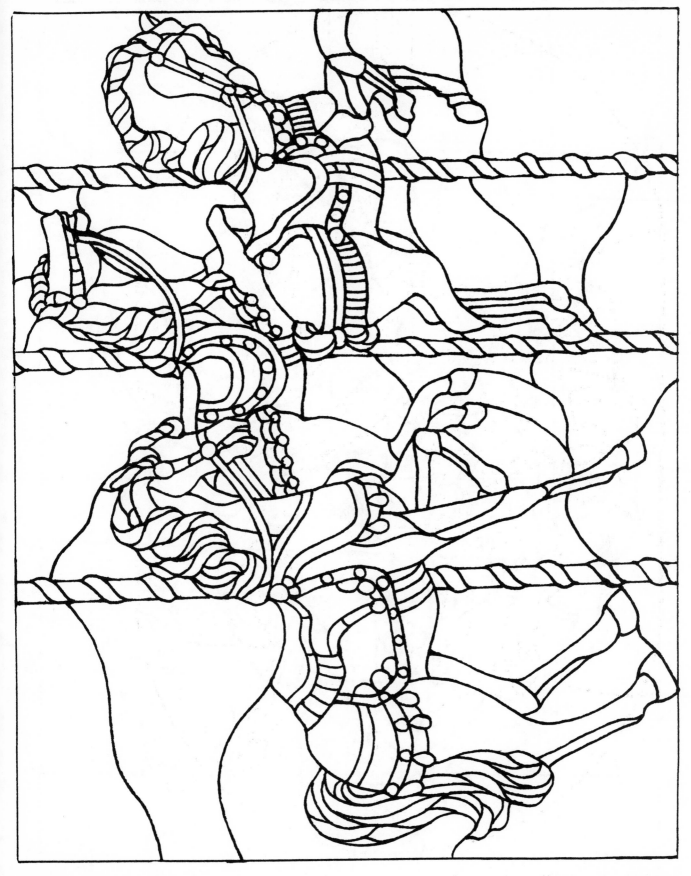

TM-42   Carousel Horses, Three in Profile

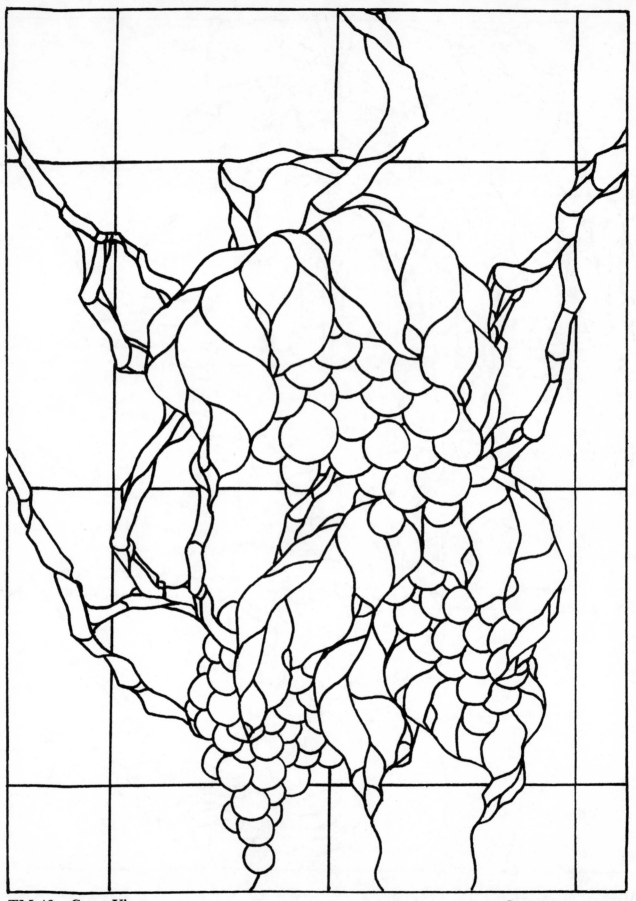

TM-43   Grape Vine

TM-44 Cattails

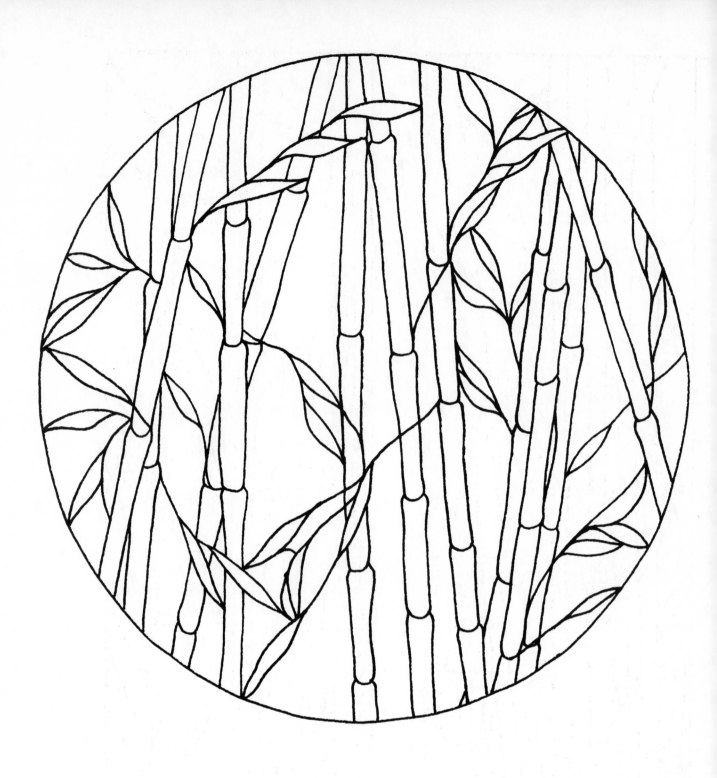

TM-45 Bamboo

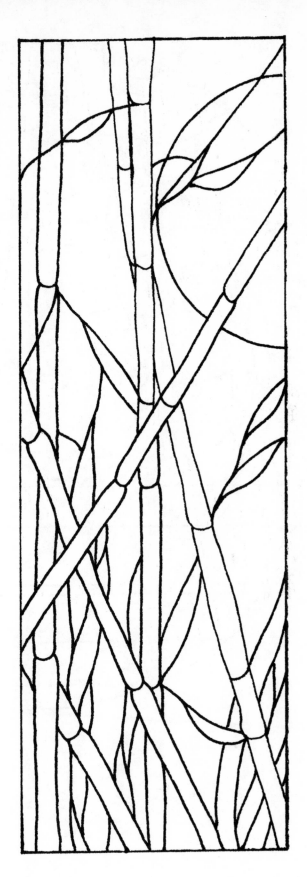

TM-46   Bamboo Side Lites, Two

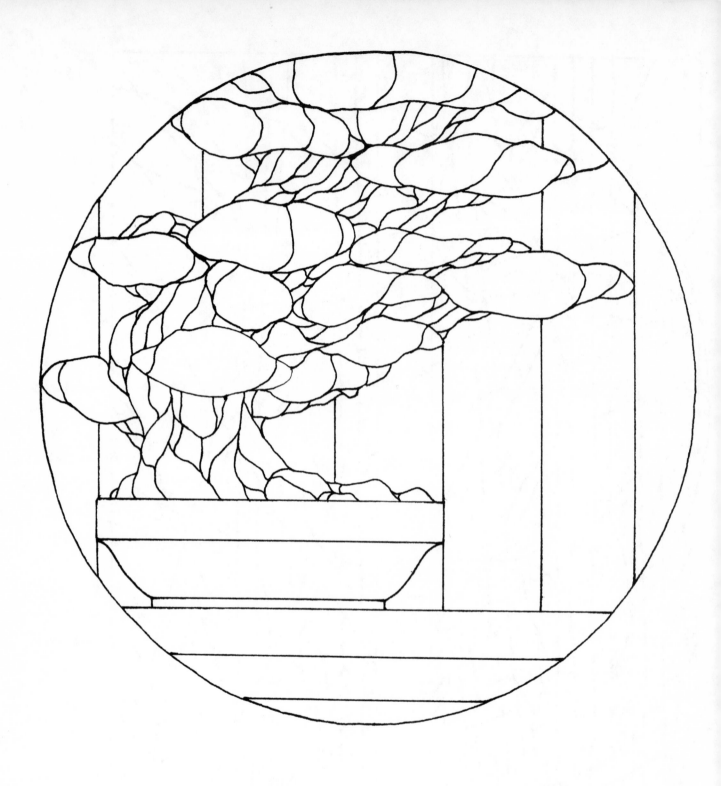

TM-47   Bonsai Cypress

TM-48   Volcano in the Wave

TM-49 Sailboat Running

TM-50 Tropical Lagoon

© 1985, Aurora Publications

TM-51   Beach Scene

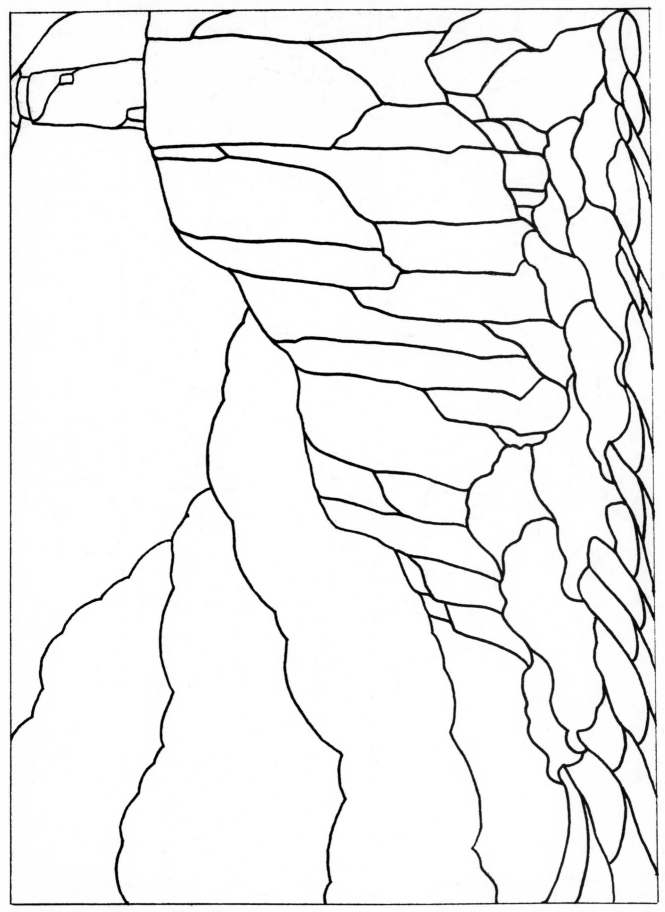

TM-52 Light House on the Rocks

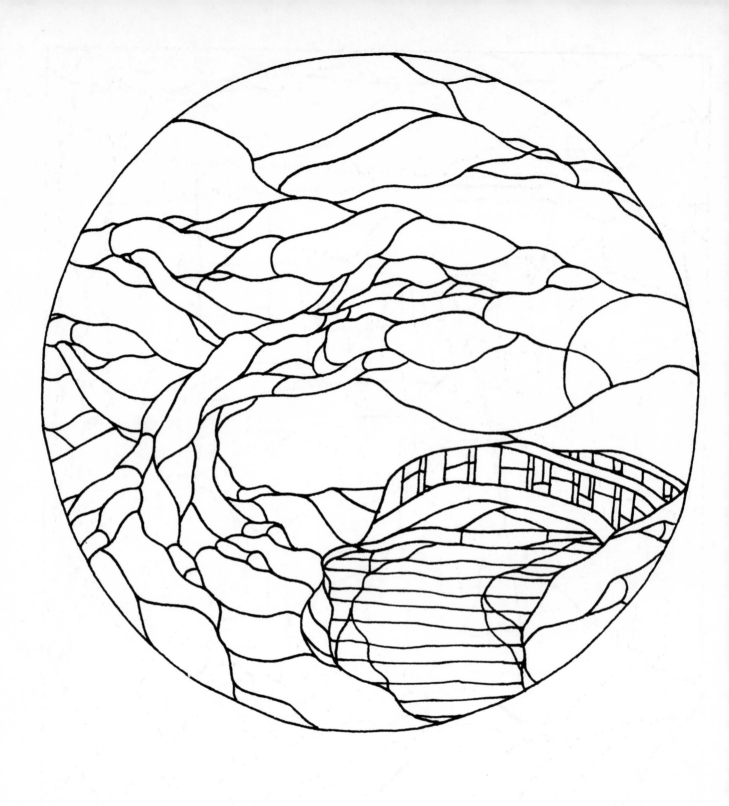

TM-53   Tree Over River and Bridge

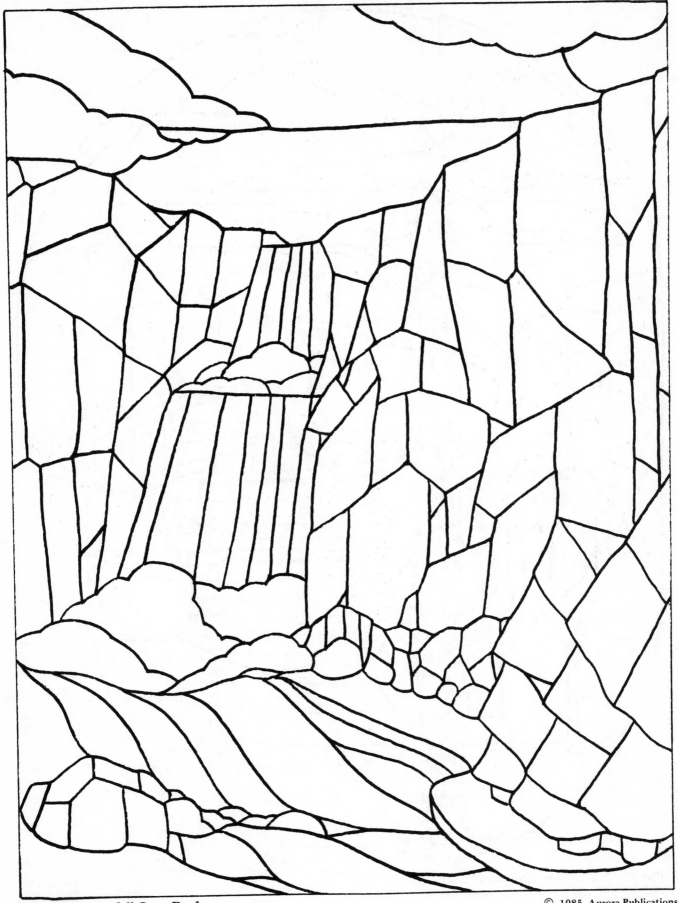

TM-54   Waterfall Over Rocks

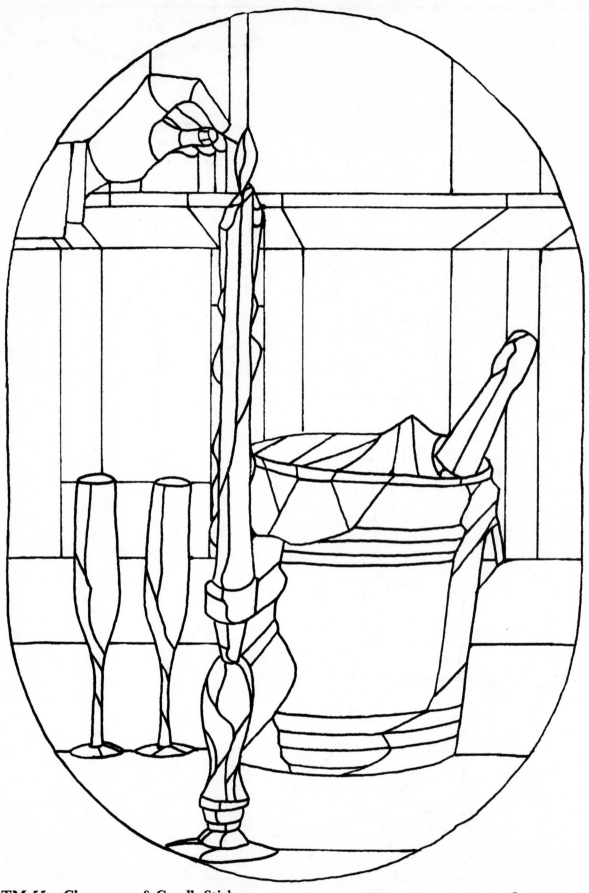

TM-55 Champagne & Candle Stick

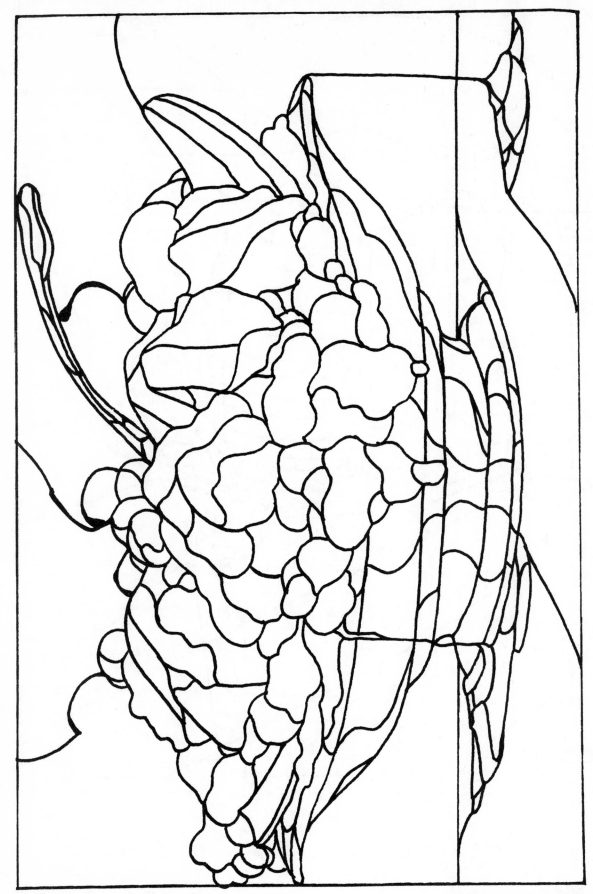

TM-56   **Banana Split Sundae**

© 1985, Aurora Publications

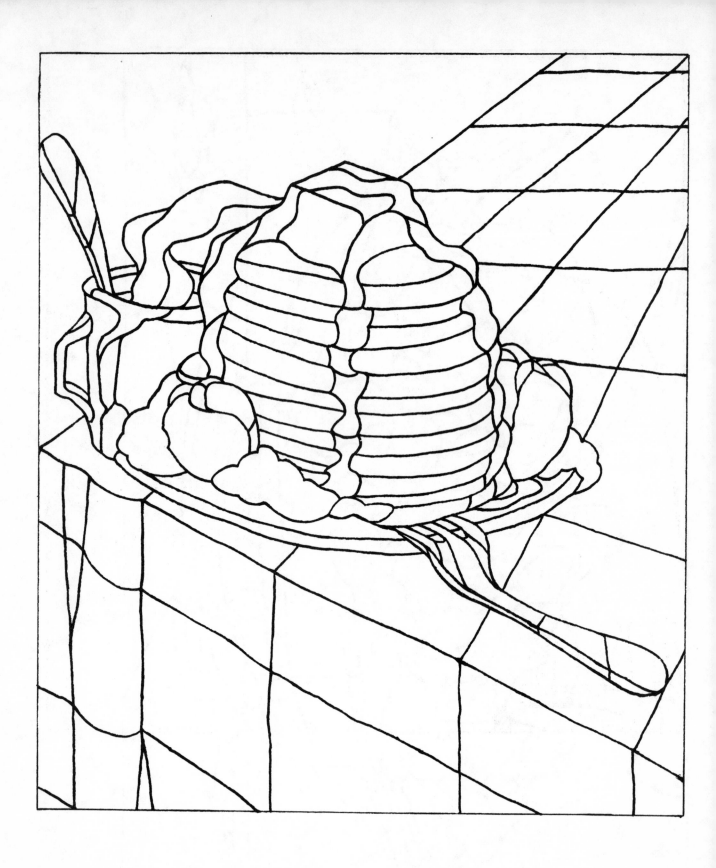

TM-57   Pancakes and Coffee Breakfast

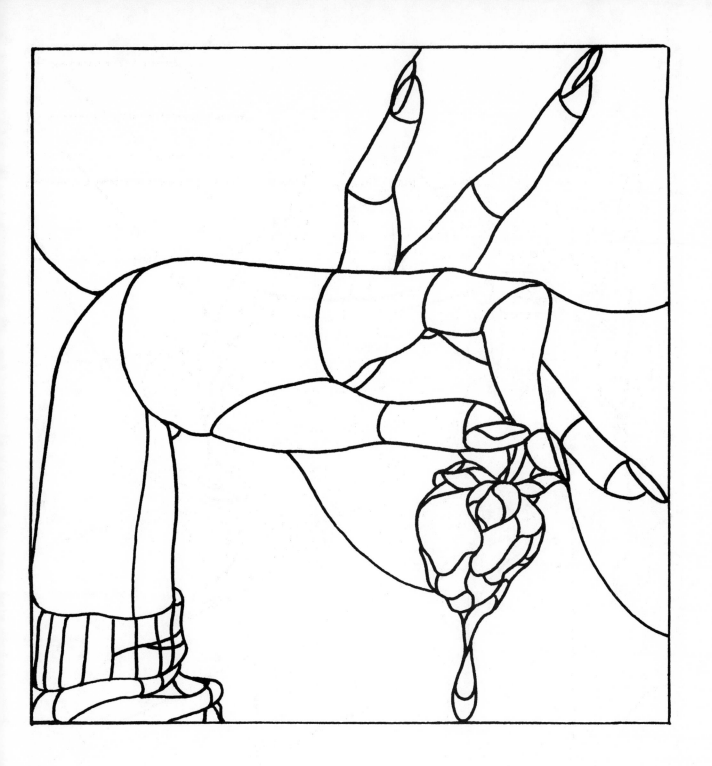

TM-58   Strawberry in Hand

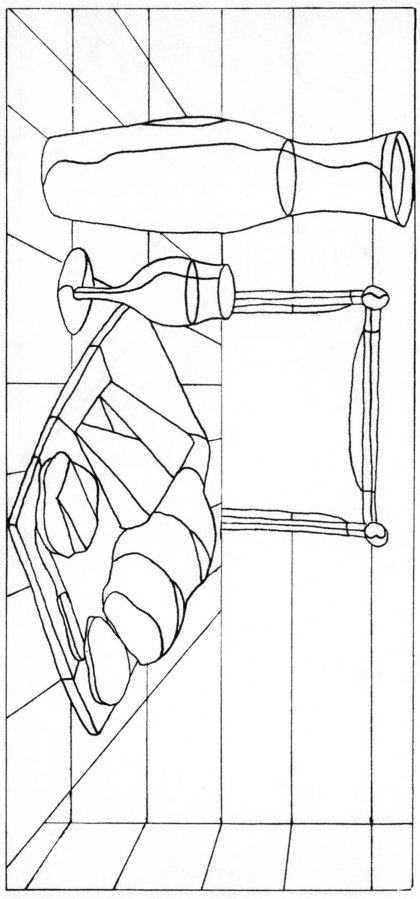

TM-59   Jug of Wine, Cheese and Bread

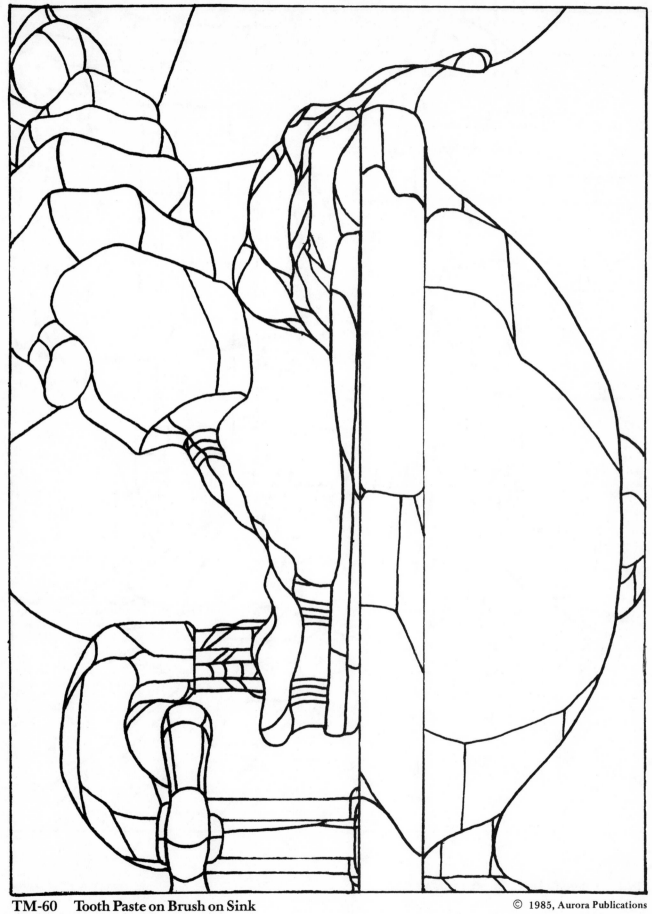

TM-60   Tooth Paste on Brush on Sink

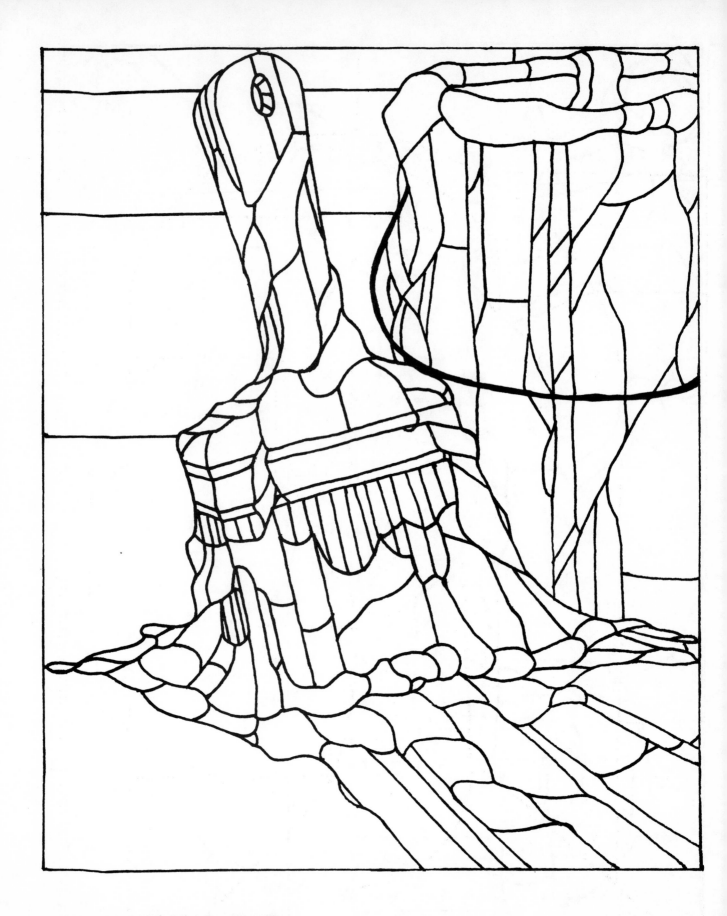

TM-61 Colorful Paint Brush and Can

TM-62   Lady in the Castle Hall

© 1985, Aurora Publications

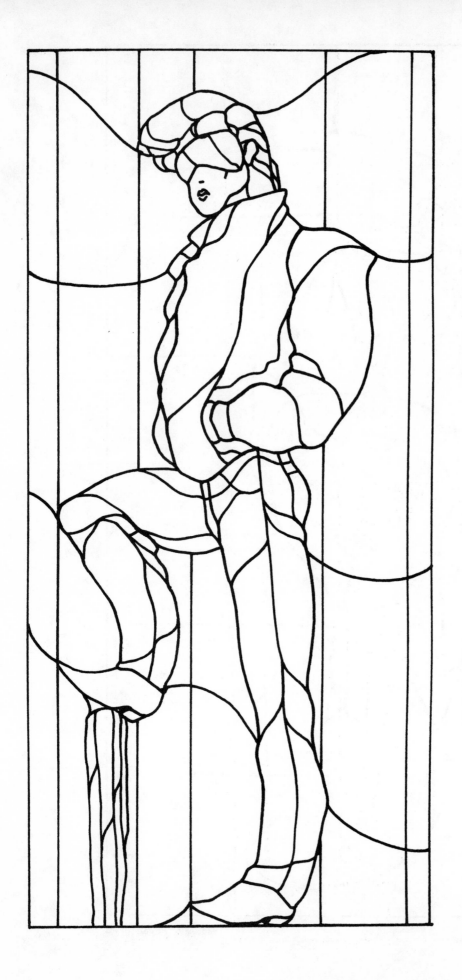

TM-63   Cowboy

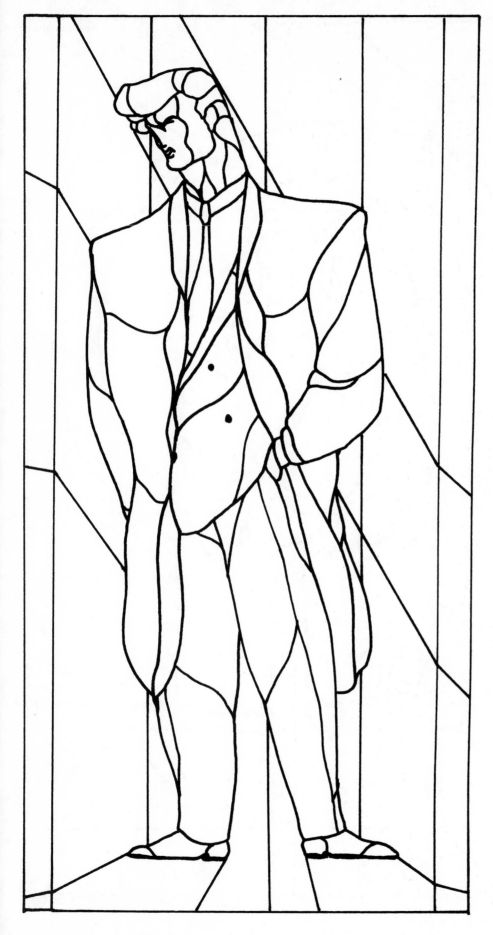

TM-64 Highrise Executive

TM-65   Sun Worshipper

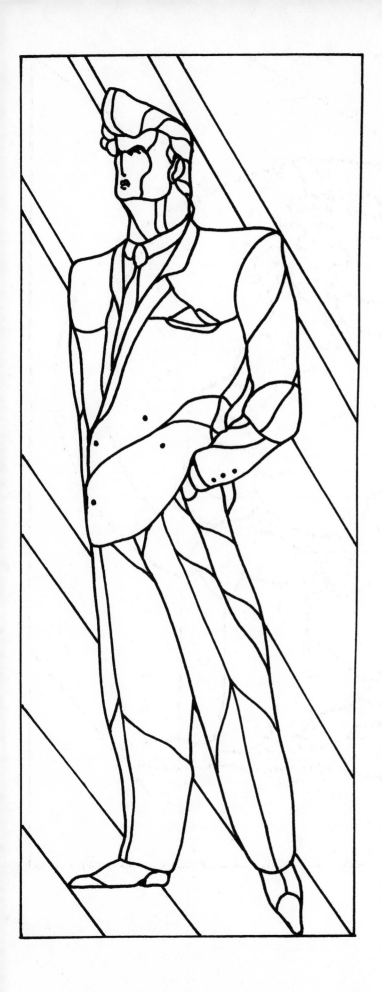

TM-66   7th Avenue Power Broker

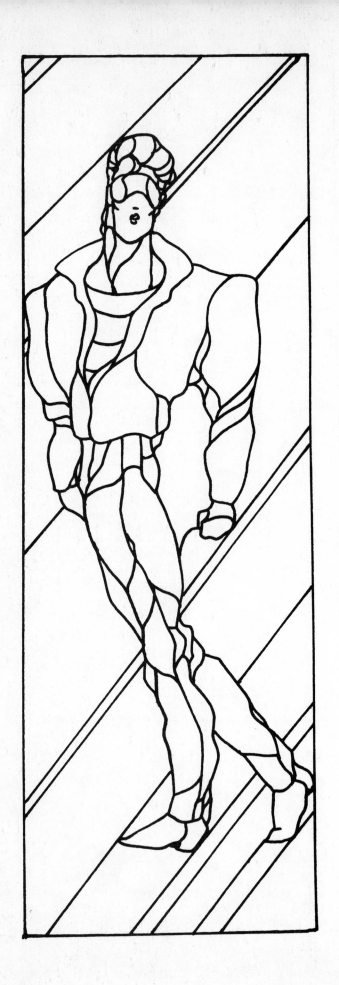

TM-67   Casual Walker